TABLE OF CONTENTS:

CHAPTER 1: MEXICAN RECIPES 7

- MEXICAN CAPIROTADA 8
- BAKED CORN TORTILLA STRIPS FOR MEXICAN SOUPS 10
- MEXICAN-STYLE SWEET CORNBREAD 12
- STUFFED GREEN PEPPERS 14
- MEXICAN POT ROAST 16
- TACO SALAD 18
- MEXICAN CEVICHE 20
- MEXICAN CHARRED TOMATILLO SALSA 22
- RICE & BEEF TACOS 24
- MEXICAN CORN-OFF-THE-COB SALAD 26
- MEXICAN PIZZA 28
- MEXICAN HASH 30
- CHORIZO BREAKFAST PIE 32
- MEXICAN BEANS 35
- BLACK BEANS AND RICE 37
- MEXICAN TINGA 39
- MEXICAN SHREDDED CHUCK ROAST 41
- MEXICAN TACO MEATLOAF 44
- TRADITIONAL MEXICAN MOLLETES 46
- MEXICAN CHICKEN TORTILLA LASAGNA 48
- CREOLE MEXICAN CATFISH 50
- MEXICAN PAELLA WITH CAULIFLOWER RICE 52
- MEXICAN SHAKSHUKA 55
- MEXICAN POTATO SAUSAGE CASSEROLE 57
- BAKED MEXICAN CHIPS ON A STICK 59
- ORIGINAL MEXICAN SHRIMP COCKTAIL 61
- MEXICAN STEAK AND VEGGIE SALAD 63
- BURRITOS WITH MEXICAN CHORIZO AND POTATOES 66
- CHILI-LIME SHRIMP FAJITAS 68
- CALABACITAS GUISADA 70
- MEXICAN PORK CHILI 72
- MEXICAN TURKEY BURGERS 75
- SOPA DE TORTILLA 77
- VEGAN MEXICAN MENUDO 79

SEITAN FAJITAS	82
HOMEMADE CHICKEN FAJITAS	84
RANCH-STYLE FAJITAS	87
VEGAN FAJITAS	89
SHRIMP QUESADILLAS	91
THANKSGIVING QUESADILLA	94
CREAMY JALAPENO AND PULLED PORK QUESADILLA	96
HAM, EGG, AND CHEESE QUESADILLAS	98
CHICKEN QUESADILLAS	100
VEGAN BLACK BEAN QUESADILLAS	102
JALAPENO AND CANADIAN BACON BREAKFAST QUESADILLAS	104
APPLE-CINNAMON BURRITO	107
GARBANZO BEAN AND VEGGIE BURRITOS	109

MEXICAN COOKBOOK 2021

BRIAN DAVISON

Brian Davison

© Copyright 2021 by Brian Davison All rights reserved.

The following Book is reproduced below with the goal of providing information that is as accurate and reliable as possible. Regardless, purchasing this Book can be seen as consent to the fact that both the publisher and the author of this book are in no way experts on the topics discussed within and that any recommendations or suggestions that are made herein are for entertainment purposes only. Professionals should be consulted as needed prior to undertaking any of the action endorsed herein.

This declaration is deemed fair and valid by both the American Bar Association and the Committee of Publishers Association and is legally binding throughout the United States.

Furthermore, the transmission, duplication, or reproduction of any of the following work including specific information will be considered an illegal act irrespective of if it is done electronically or in print. This extends to creating a secondary or tertiary copy of the work or a recorded copy and is only allowed with the express written consent from the Publisher. All additional right reserved.

The information in the following pages is broadly considered a truthful and accurate account of facts and as such, any inattention, use, or misuse of the information in question by the reader will render any resulting actions solely under their purview. There are no scenarios in which the publisher or the original author of this work can be in any fashion deemed liable for any hardship or damages that may befall them after undertaking information described herein.

Additionally, the information in the following pages is intended only for informational purposes and should thus be thought of as universal.

As befitting its nature, it is presented without assurance regarding its prolonged validity or interim quality. Trademarks that are mentioned are done without written consent and can in no way be considered an endorsement from the trademark holder.

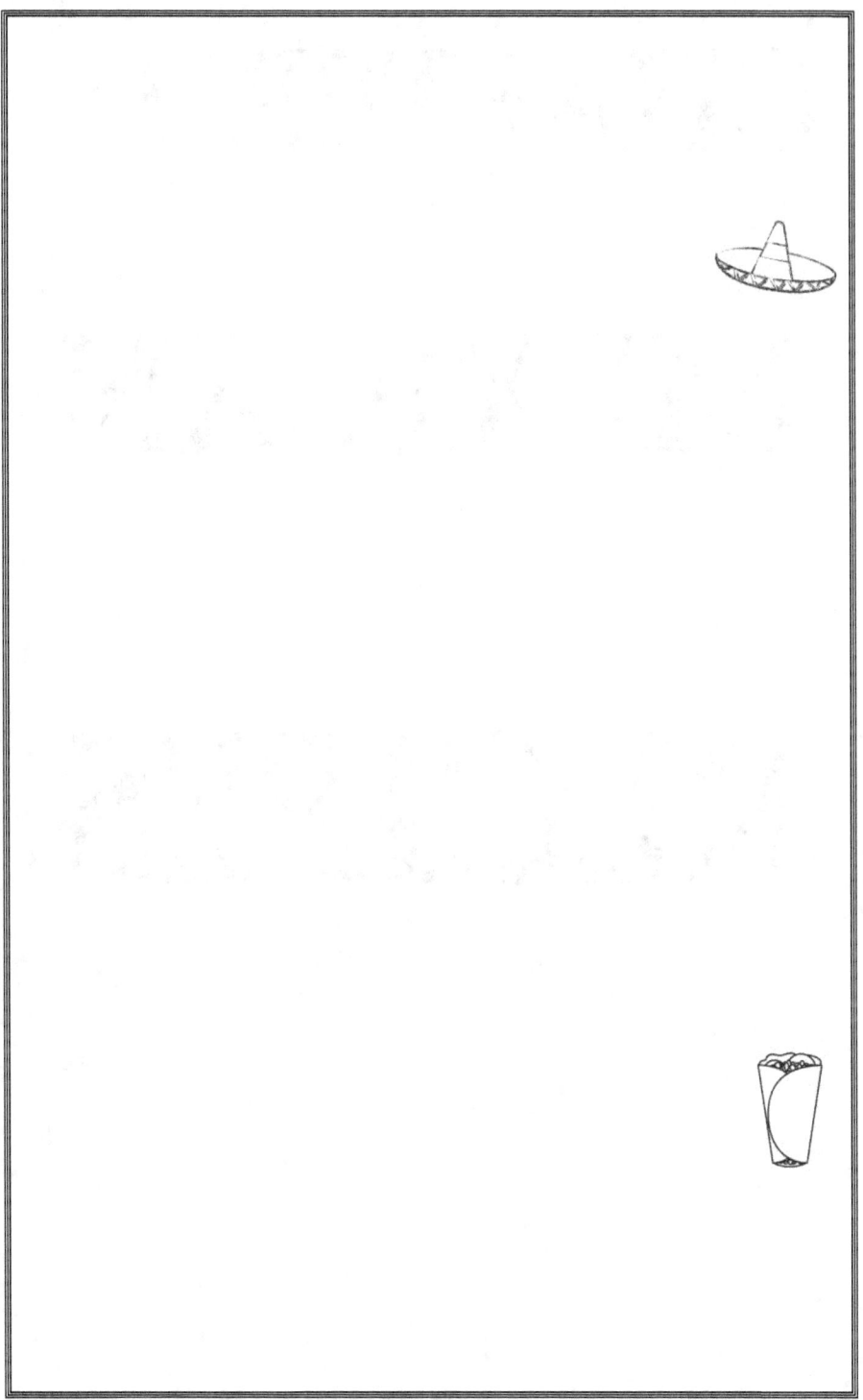

CHAPTER 1: MEXICAN RECIPES

MEXICAN CAPIROTADA

Prep:
15 mins
Cook:
45 mins
Additional:
20 mins
Total:
80 mins
Servings:
24
Yield:
24 servings

INGREDIENTS:

3 cups water
3 cups brown sugar, divided
2 cinnamon sticks
2 cups butter, softened
2 loaves sliced white bread, toasted
¼ teaspoon ground cinnamon, or to taste
¼ teaspoon ground nutmeg, or to taste
⅛ teaspoon ground cloves, or to taste
2 cups raisins
2 cups peanuts
1 pound shredded sharp Cheddar cheese

DIRECTIONS:

1

Preheat oven to 350 degrees F (175 degrees C).

2

Combine water, 2 cups brown sugar, and cinnamon sticks together in a saucepan; bring to a boil. Reduce heat and simmer, stirring occasionally, until sugar is dissolved and liquid has reduced into a syrup, about 15 minutes. Remove cinnamon sticks from syrup using a slotted spoon.

3

Spread butter onto each toasted bread slice. Make 1 layer of buttered bread in a deep casserole dish or oven-proof stockpot. Sprinkle cinnamon, nutmeg, and cloves over bread layer. Sprinkle 1/4 the raisins, 1/4 the peanuts, 1/4 the remaining brown sugar, and 1/4 the Cheddar cheese over bread layer. Repeat layering with remaining ingredients. Pour cinnamon syrup over entire dish; cover with aluminum foil.

4

Bake in the preheated oven until cooked through, about 30 minutes. Cool for 20 minutes before serving.

NUTRITION FACTS:

490 calories; protein 11g; carbohydrates 49.6g; fat 29g; cholesterol 60.5mg; sodium 590.3mg

BAKED CORN TORTILLA STRIPS FOR MEXICAN SOUPS

Prep:
5 mins
Cook:
15 mins
Total:
20 mins
Servings:
4
Yield:
4 servings

INGREDIENTS:

8 (6 inch) corn tortillas
2 tablespoons avocado oil, or more as needed

DIRECTIONS:

1

Preheat the oven to 350 degrees F (175 degrees C).

2

Cut tortillas first in half, then crosswise into 1/8-inch strips. Place in a bowl and toss with oil until fully coated. Arrange tortilla strips in a single layer on a baking sheet.

3

Bake in the preheated oven until strips are crisp and lightly browned, about 15 minutes. Remove from the oven and cool.

NUTRITION FACTS:

175 calories; protein 3g; carbohydrates 23.2g; fat 8.5g; sodium 23.4mg

MEXICAN-STYLE SWEET CORNBREAD

Prep:
5 mins
Cook:
45 mins
Total:
50 mins
Servings:
8
Yield:
8 servings

INGREDIENTS:

¼ cup white sugar
¼ cup water
¼ teaspoon salt
1 (8.5 ounce) package dry corn muffin mix
1 (14.25 ounce) can sweet cream-style corn
¼ cup butter, melted

DIRECTIONS:

1

Preheat the oven to 350 degrees F (175 degrees C). Grease a 9x5-inch loaf pan.

2

Combine corn muffin mix, corn, butter, sugar, water, and salt in a bowl. Pour into the greased loaf pan.

3

Bake in the preheated oven until all the liquid is absorbed, 45 to 50 minutes. Scoop onto serving dishes with an ice cream scoop.

NUTRITION FACTS:

237 calories; protein 3g; carbohydrates 36.3g; fat 9.6g; cholesterol 15.9mg; sodium 592.4mg.

STUFFED GREEN PEPPERS

Prep:
20 mins
Cook:
1 hr 10 mins
Total:
1 hr 30 mins
Servings:
4
Yield:
4 stuffed peppers

INGREDIENTS:

1 pound ground beef
⅔ cup water
1 (1 ounce) package taco seasoning
2 cups hot cooked instant white rice, or as needed
1 (10.75 ounce) can condensed tomato soup
1 tomato, chopped
1 cup finely chopped mushrooms
¼ cup chopped red onion
¼ cup crumbled feta cheese
¼ cup chopped green onions
4 green bell peppers, tops and seeds removed
2 tablespoons kalamata olives, or to taste

DIRECTIONS:

1

Preheat oven to 350 degrees F (175 degrees C).

2

Heat a large skillet over medium-high heat. Cook and stir beef in the hot skillet until browned and crumbly, 5 to 7 minutes; drain and discard grease. Add water and taco seasoning to ground beef; cook and stir until until water evaporates, about 5 minutes.

3

Mix ground beef mixture, rice, tomato soup, tomato, mushrooms, red onion, feta cheese, and green onions together in a bowl; spoon into green bell peppers. Arrange stuffed peppers in a baking dish.

4

Bake in the preheated oven until peppers are softened and filling is cooked through, about 1 hour. Serve with kalamata olives on the side.

NUTRITION FACTS:

515 calories; protein 26.4g; carbohydrates 46.1g; fat 24.8g; cholesterol 83.7mg; sodium 1308mg.

MEXICAN POT ROAST

Prep:
15 mins
Cook:
8 hrs 10 mins
Total:
8 hrs 25 mins
Servings:
12
Yield:
12 servings

INGREDIENTS:

2 tablespoons olive oil
1 (4 pound) beef chuck roast, trimmed
1 teaspoon salt
1 teaspoon ground black pepper
1 large onion, chopped
1 ¼ cups diced green chile pepper
1 (5 ounce) bottle hot sauce
¼ cup taco seasoning
1 teaspoon chili powder
1 teaspoon cayenne pepper
1 teaspoon garlic powder

DIRECTIONS:

1
Heat olive oil in a large skillet over medium-high heat. Season beef chuck roast with salt and pepper. Cook roast in hot oil until browned entirely, 2 to 3 minutes per side; transfer browned roast to a slow cooker.

2
Sprinkle onion, chile pepper, hot sauce, taco seasoning, chili powder, cayenne pepper, and garlic powder over the roast.

3
Cook on Low until meat is fall-apart tender, 8 to 10 hours.

NUTRITION FACTS:

213 calories; protein 21.2g; carbohydrates 5.4g; fat 11.2g; cholesterol 70.2mg; sodium 771.9mg.

TACO SALAD

Prep:
25 mins
Cook:
20 mins
Total:
45 mins
Servings:
6
Yield:
6 servings

INGREDIENTS:

2 teaspoons olive oil
1 large onion, finely chopped
3 cloves garlic, minced
1 pound ground turkey
1 (19 ounce) can kidney beans, rinsed and drained
1 cup salsa
2 cups shredded iceberg lettuce
2 small carrots, julienned
2 red bell peppers, cut into thin strips
2 tablespoons chili powder
2 teaspoons ground cumin
1 teaspoon dried oregano
1 dash cayenne pepper

DIRECTIONS:

1

Heat the olive oil in a skillet over medium heat. Stir in the onion and garlic; cook and stir until the onion has softened and turned translucent, about 5 minutes. Add the turkey, and stir until crumbly and no longer pink. Season with chili powder, cumin, oregano, cayenne pepper, kidney beans, and salsa. Cook over medium-high heat until the mixture is simmering and the beans are hot, about 5 minutes.

2

Divide the lettuce, carrots, and red bell peppers among 4 serving plates. Spoon the turkey mixture overtop to serve.

NUTRITION FACTS:

300 calories; protein 27.7g; carbohydrates 25.7g; fat 10.7g; cholesterol 77mg; sodium 553.1mg.

MEXICAN CEVICHE

Prep:
30 mins
Cook:
30 mins
Additional:
1 hr
Total:
1 hr 60 mins
Servings:
8
Yield:
8 servings

INGREDIENTS:

5 large lemons, juiced
1 pound jumbo shrimp, peeled and deveined
¼ cup chopped fresh cilantro, or to taste
tomato and clam juice cocktail
2 white onions, finely chopped
1 cucumber, peeled and finely chopped
1 large tomatoes, seeded and chopped
3 fresh jalapeno peppers, seeded and minced
1 bunch radishes, finely diced
2 cloves fresh garlic, minced
tortilla chips

DIRECTIONS:

1

Place shrimp in a bowl (You may either coarsely chop the shrimp, or leave them whole, depending on your preference.)
Add lemon, covering shrimp completely. Cover, and refrigerate for 30 minutes, or until opaque and slightly firm.

2

Add tomatoes, onions, cucumber, radishes, and garlic; toss to combine. Gradually add cilantro and jalapenos to desired taste (jalapeno will grow stronger while marinating). Stir in tomato and clam juices to desired consistency. Cover, and refrigerate for 1 hour. Serve chilled with tortilla chips.

NUTRITION FACTS:

387 calories; protein 17.7g; carbohydrates 57.6g; fat 12.4g; cholesterol 86.3mg; sodium 732.5mg.

MEXICAN CHARRED TOMATILLO SALSA

Prep:
15 mins
Cook:
11 mins
Total:
26 mins
Servings:
8
Yield:
8 servings

INGREDIENTS:

2 pounds fresh tomatillos, husks removed
10 dried chile de arbol peppers
2 cloves garlic, unpeeled
salt to taste

DIRECTIONS:

1

Line a heavy cast iron grill pan or griddle with aluminum foil and place over high heat. Arrange tomatillos, chiles de arbol, and garlic in a single layer on top.
Grill until chiles
are blackened, turning as necessary, 3 to 5 minutes. Transfer to a bowl. Continue grilling tomatillos and garlic until they are evenly blackened, 8 to 10 minutes more.

2

Peel garlic and place in a mortar and pestle. Season with salt and pound into a thick paste. Add chiles; pound until smooth. Add as many tomatillos as you can fit in your mortar; pound until chunky. Transfer salsa to a bowl. Repeat with remaining tomatillos, mixing them into the bowl of salsa in batches.

NUTRITION FACTS:

40 calories; protein 1.2g; carbohydrates 7.3g; fat 1.2g; sodium 20.9mg.

RICE & BEEF TACOS

Prep:
19 mins
Cook:
20 mins
Total:
39 mins
Servings:
4
Yield:
4 servings

INGREDIENTS:

2 tablespoons Butter Spread, divided
1 pound lean ground beef
1 green or red bell pepper, chopped
1 medium red onion, chopped
2 cups water
1 (5.4 ounce) package Mexican Rice
1 medium tomato, chopped
8 taco shells

DIRECTIONS:

1
Melt 1 tablespoon Spread in large nonstick skillet over medium-high heat and brown ground beef,
seasoned with salt and pepper, if desired;
remove and set aside.

2
Melt remaining 1 tablespoon Spread in same skillet over medium-high heat and cook peppers and onions, stirring occasionally, until crisp-tender, about 5 minutes. Stir in water, Mexican Rice and tomato and bring to a boil over high heat. Reduce heat and simmer, covered, 7 minutes or until rice is tender.

3
Stir in beef; heat through. Spoon into taco shells and serve, if desired, with lime wedges. Top, if desired, with your favorite taco toppings such as sour cream, chopped red onion and shredded lettuce.

NUTRITION FACTS:

613 calories; protein 29.8g; carbohydrates 41.1g; fat 27.8g; cholesterol 79mg; sodium 307.1mg.

MEXICAN CORN-OFF-THE-COB SALAD

Prep:
15 mins
Cook:
15 mins
Total:
30 mins
Servings:
6
Yield:
6 servings

INGREDIENTS:

4 ears corn, with husks
½ lime, juiced, or more to taste
½ teaspoon chili powder
5 ounces crumbled cotija cheese
¼ cup packed chopped fresh cilantro
4 tablespoons mayonnaise
1 pinch ground black pepper to taste
1 pinch salt to taste

DIRECTIONS:

1
Preheat an outdoor grill for medium-high heat and lightly oil the grate.

2
Grill corn in the husks on the preheated grill, turning occasionally, to desired tenderness, about 15 minutes; some charring is fine. Remove from the grill. Remove and discard husks and silk when cool enough to handle. Cut kernels off into a medium bowl.

3
Add lime juice and chili powder, then mix in cotija cheese, cilantro, mayonnaise, and pepper until thoroughly combined. Taste and add salt if necessary.

NUTRITION FACTS:

209 calories; protein 7.2g; carbohydrates 13.7g; fat 15.2g; cholesterol 28.3mg; sodium 357.6mg.

MEXICAN PIZZA

Prep:
20 mins
Cook:
12 mins
Total:
32 mins
Servings:
6
Yield:
6 slices

INGREDIENTS:

½ (16 ounce) can spicy fat-free beans
1 cup salsa, divided
1 (12 inch) pre-baked Italian pizza crust
2 cups shredded hearts of romaine lettuce
3 medium green onions, thinly sliced
¼ cup ranch dressing
¼ cup crumbled tortilla chips
1 cup shredded pepper Jack or Monterey Jack cheese

DIRECTIONS:

1

Adjust oven rack to lowest position, and heat oven to 450 degrees.
Mix beans and 1/2 cup salsa in a medium bowl.
Place crust on a cookie sheet,
then spread the bean mixture over crust.
Bake until it's crisp and warm, about 10 minutes.

2

Remove from oven; top with lettuce, green onions and dollop with the remaining salsa. Drizzle (or, if dressing has an easy-pour top, squirt) dressing over pizza. Top with chips and cheese, then return to oven and bake until the cheese melts, about 2 minutes longer. Cut into 6 slices and serve.

NUTRITION FACTS:

373 calories; protein 17g; carbohydrates 44g; fat 15.3g; cholesterol 26.1mg; sodium 1026.7mg

MEXICAN HASH

Prep:
5 mins
Cook:
25 mins
Total:
30 mins
Servings:
4
Yield:
4 servings

INGREDIENTS:

12 ounces uncooked chorizo sausage
¼ cup chopped onion
2 teaspoons vegetable oil
1 (16 ounce) package frozen diced hash brown potatoes
½ teaspoon seasoning salt
1 (14.5 ounce) can Diced Tomatoes, drained
2 tablespoons coarsely chopped cilantro
1 avocado, cubed

DIRECTIONS:

1

Heat a skillet over medium-high heat. Add chorizo, breaking it apart until crumbly. Saute until it starts to brown, about 3 minutes. Add chopped onion and cook, stirring frequently, until onion is translucent, about 3 minutes. Transfer chorizo-onion mixture to a plate.

2

Pour oil into pan and heat over medium-high heat. Add frozen hash brown potatoes and seasoning salt. Stir to coat potatoes in the oil.

3

Let the potatoes brown on one side, then flip once after about 5 minutes. Both sides should be browned and crispy, about 5 minutes per side. Add the diced tomatoes and the chorizo and onion mixture; stir gently to mix evenly. Cook for 4 more minutes, stirring once to rotate the ingredients from the bottom of the pan to the top for even cooking.

4

Serve topped with cilantro and cubed avocados.

NUTRITION FACTS:

599 calories; protein 24.7g; carbohydrates 31.1g; fat 49.1g;

CHORIZO BREAKFAST PIE

Prep:
15 mins
Cook:
1 hr 25 mins
Total:
1 hr 40 mins
Servings:
8
Yield:
1 9-inch pie

INGREDIENTS:

3 cups frozen shredded hash browns
3 large eggs eggs, beaten, divided
2 tablespoons minced onion
1 tablespoon all-purpose flour
1 teaspoon salt
1 ½ tablespoons olive oil
1 pound bulk Mexican chorizo sausage
1 onion, chopped
2 cloves garlic, minced
¼ cup milk
2 tablespoons chopped fresh cilantro
1 teaspoon ground cumin
1 ½ cups shredded Monterey Jack cheese

DIRECTIONS:

1
Preheat the oven to 400 degrees F (200 degrees C). Grease a 9-inch pie pan.

2
Combine hash browns, 1 egg, minced onion, flour, and salt in a bowl. Pour into the prepared pie pan and smooth down to form a crust.

3
Bake in the preheated oven for 30 minutes. Brush the crust with olive oil and continue to bake until golden and set, about 10 minutes more. Remove from the oven and reduce temperature to 350 degrees F (175 degrees C).

4
Heat a large skillet over medium-high heat. Cook and stir chorizo in the hot skillet until browned and crumbly, 5 to 7 minutes. Add chopped onion and garlic and saute for another 3 minutes. Remove any extra grease from the pan if desired.

5
Beat remaining eggs and milk together in a bowl until smooth; add cilantro and cumin.

6
Spread half of the Monterey Jack cheese onto the potato crust. Spoon chorizo mixture over and top with remaining Monterey Jack cheese. Pour egg mixture over the top.

7
Bake in the preheated oven until eggs are set and the top of the pie is slightly browned, 35 to 40 minutes. Serve warm.

NUTRITION FACTS:

399 calories; protein 20.3g; carbohydrates 14.5g; fat 28.8g; cholesterol 129.1mg; sodium 1008.5mg.

MEXICAN BEANS

Prep:
20 mins
Cook:
4 hrs
Total:
4 hrs 20 mins
Servings:
24
Yield:
24 servings

INGREDIENTS:

2 pounds dried pinto beans
2 ½ quarts water
1 pound bacon, coarsely chopped
1 medium onion, chopped
1 medium ripe tomato, chopped
1 fresh jalapeno pepper, chopped
1 bunch fresh cilantro, chopped

DIRECTIONS:

1

Combine beans and water in a large pot. Bring to a boil, reduce heat, and simmer for 3 hours. Add more water if necessary while beans are cooking.

2

In a large skillet, cook bacon over medium heat until it is beginning to brown. Stir in onion, and continue cooking until onion is tender. Stir in tomato, and jalapeno, and cook for 2 to 3 minutes. Remove from heat, and stir in cilantro.

3

Stir bacon and onion mixture into the beans, and continue cooking for 1 hour, or until beans are soft.

NUTRITION FACTS:

221 calories; protein 10.5g; carbohydrates 24.5g; fat 9g; cholesterol 12.9mg; sodium 166.6mg

BLACK BEANS AND RICE

Prep:
10 mins
Cook:
20 mins
Total:
30 mins
Servings:
4
Yield:
4 servings

INGREDIENTS:

2 tablespoons coconut oil
1 teaspoon chili powder
1 teaspoon garlic powder
1 teaspoon ground cumin
1 teaspoon ground coriander
2 stalks celery, chopped
1 tomato, chopped
½ cup frozen corn
2 teaspoons chopped fresh oregano
2 teaspoons chopped fresh cilantro
1 (15 ounce) can black beans, rinsed and drained
½ cup mild salsa
¼ cup water, or as needed
2 cups cooked white rice
salt to taste

DIRECTIONS:

1

Heat coconut oil in a large skillet over medium-low heat. Add chili powder, garlic powder, cumin, and coriander; fry until fragrant, about 30 seconds. Add celery, cook and stir until softened, 3 to 5 minutes.

2

Add tomato, frozen corn, oregano, and cilantro; stir to coat. Stir in black beans and salsa. Bring to a simmer and cook for 10 to 15 minutes, adding water as needed to keep the mixture saucy.

3

Remove from the heat and stir in cooked rice until coated. Season with salt.

NUTRITION FACTS:

304 calories; protein 10.5g; carbohydrates 49.7g; fat 8g; sodium 668.8mg

MEXICAN TINGA

Prep:
10 mins
Cook:
25 mins
Total:
35 mins
Servings:
8
Yield:
16 tingas

INGREDIENTS:

2 tablespoons olive oil
1 large onion, cut into rings
1 (15 ounce) can stewed tomatoes
1 (7 ounce) can chipotle peppers in adobo sauce, or to taste
2 pounds shredded cooked chicken meat
16 tostada shells
½ cup sour cream

DIRECTIONS:

1

Heat olive oil in a saucepan over medium heat. Add the onions; cook and stir until softened and translucent, about 5 minutes. Meanwhile, puree the tomatoes with chipotle peppers and adobo sauce to taste. Pour into the onions, and add chicken. Cover, and simmer for 20 minutes.

2

To serve, mound the chicken onto tostada shells, and garnish with a dollop of sour cream.

NUTRITION FACTS:

402 calories; protein 33.6g; carbohydrates 20.5g; fat 20g; cholesterol 91.4mg; sodium 395.5mg.

MEXICAN SHREDDED CHUCK ROAST

Prep:
15 mins
Cook:
2 hrs 55 mins
Total:
2 hrs 70 mins
Servings:
12
Yield:
12 servings

INGREDIENTS:

1 (3 pound) beef chuck roast
salt and ground black pepper to taste
2 tablespoons grapeseed oil
1 large onion, diced
4 cloves garlic, minced
1 (14 ounce) can beef broth, divided
1 (12 ounce) bottle Mexican guajillo red chile cooking sauce
3 bay leaves

DIRECTIONS:

1

Preheat the oven to 325 degrees F (165 degrees C).

2

Cut chuck roast into 3-inch cubes, removing excess fat and connective tissue. Season beef with salt and pepper.

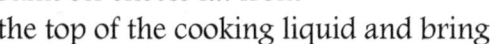

3

Heat grapeseed oil in a large Dutch oven over high heat. Sear cubes of beef a few at a time, until well browned on all sides, about 4 minutes per batch. Reserve browned beef in a bowl. Reduce heat to medium and add onion and garlic. Cook until soft and just beginning to brown, about 10 minutes.

4

Add 1 cup beef broth to onion mixture and stir well; simmer for 1 to 2 minutes. Add beef and pour in guajillo sauce. Add a little beef broth to the empty jar, seal, and shake to release remaining sauce; pour over the beef. Pour in enough of the remaining broth to just cover the beef. Add bay leaves and bring to a gentle simmer.

5

Bake in the preheated oven, covered, until beef is fork-tender, about 2 1/2 hours.

6

Remove beef from sauce and set aside; discard bay leaves. Skim off excess fat from the top of the cooking liquid and bring to a boil to reduce slightly. Shred beef with two forks and return to cooking sauce.

NUTRITION FACTS:

207 calories; protein 14.9g; carbohydrates 4g; fat 14.3g; cholesterol 51.7mg; sodium 153.7mg.

MEXICAN TACO MEATLOAF

Prep:
15 mins
Cook:
45 mins
Total:
60 mins
Servings:
8
Yield:
1 loaf

INGREDIENTS:

1 ½ pounds lean ground beef
1 cup crushed tortilla chips
¾ cup shredded pepper Jack cheese
1 small onion, chopped
1 (1 ounce) packet taco seasoning mix
2 eggs, beaten
½ cup milk
¼ cup mild red taco sauce, or more to taste

DIRECTIONS:

1
Preheat the oven to 350 degrees F (175 degrees C).

2
Thoroughly combine beef, tortilla chips, pepper Jack cheese, onion, and taco seasoning in a bowl.

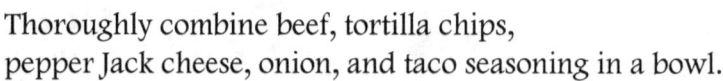

3
Whisk eggs, milk, and taco sauce together in a separate bowl. Add to meat mixture and stir until well combined.

4
Press mixture into a 9x5-inch loaf pan and top with a strip of taco sauce down the center.

5
Bake in the preheated oven until cooked through and browned on top, 45 to 60 minutes.

NUTRITION FACTS:

272 calories; protein 21.6g; carbohydrates 7.1g; fat 16.6g; cholesterol 120.2mg; sodium 468.4mg.

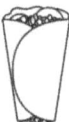

TRADITIONAL MEXICAN MOLLETES

Prep:
10 mins
Cook:
15 mins
Total:
25 mins
Servings:
4
Yield:
4 servings

INGREDIENTS:

4 bolillo rolls, sliced in half lengthwise
3 tablespoons butter, room temperature
1 (16 ounce) can refried beans, heated
1 (7 ounce) package Southwestern Cheddar & Monterey Jack Shredded Cheese
Mexican salsa or pico de gallo, for serving

DIRECTIONS:

1
Preheat oven to 400 degrees F (200 degrees C). Line a rimmed baking sheet with parchment paper.

2
Remove some of the bread from the middle of bread halves to accommodate more toppings. Spread about 1 teaspoon butter on each half.

3
Spread 2 to 3 tablespoons warmed refried beans on bread. Sprinkle about 1/4 cup Borden® Cheddar and Monterey Jack shredded cheese on the beans. Place bread halves on prepared baking sheet.

4
Bake in preheated oven until the cheese is melted and bubbly and the bread is crispy, 15 to 20 minutes.

5
Top molletes with Mexican salsa or pico de gallo.

NUTRITION FACTS:

699 calories; protein 28g; carbohydrates 85.3g; fat 26.1g; cholesterol 77.1mg; sodium 1022.5mg.

MEXICAN CHICKEN TORTILLA LASAGNA

Prep:
15 mins
Cook:
55 mins
Additional:
10 mins
Total:
80 mins
Servings:
6

INGREDIENTS:

1 tablespoon olive oil
1 small onion, diced
1 pound ground chicken
1 (10 ounce) can diced tomatoes with green chiles halfway drained
½ (1.25 ounce) package reduced-sodium taco seasoning mix
1 (10 ounce) can mild enchilada sauce, divided
5 ounces crumbled queso fresco, divided
¼ cup Mexican crema
1 tablespoon Mexican crema
1 egg
6 each corn tortillas
3 ounces grated Cheddar cheese

DIRECTIONS:

1

Preheat the oven to 375 degrees F (190 degrees C).

2

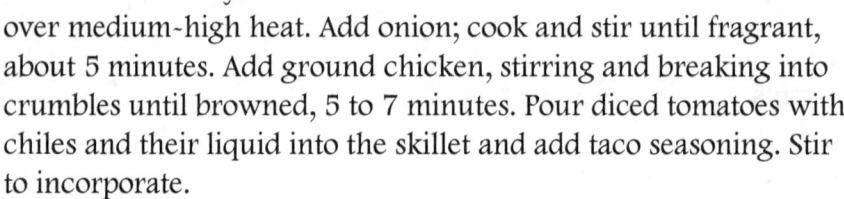

Heat oil in a heavy skillet over medium-high heat. Add onion; cook and stir until fragrant, about 5 minutes. Add ground chicken, stirring and breaking into crumbles until browned, 5 to 7 minutes. Pour diced tomatoes with chiles and their liquid into the skillet and add taco seasoning. Stir to incorporate.

3

Combine 8 ounces enchilada sauce, 4 ounces queso fresco, Mexican crema, and egg in a bowl.

4

Pour remaining enchilada sauce into the bottom of an 8x6-inch glass casserole dish. Trim tortillas to have a straight edge if desired. Lay two tortillas in the enchilada sauce in the dish. Place some chicken mixture on top and ladle some enchilada sauce mixture over. Repeat layers. Top with remaining queso fresco and Cheddar cheese.

5

Bake, covered, in the preheated oven for 35 minutes. Uncover and bake for 10 minutes more.
Let rest for 10 to 15 minutes before serving.

NUTRITION FACTS:

349 calories; protein 27.9g; carbohydrates 19.4g; fat 19.4g; cholesterol 114.3mg;

CREOLE MEXICAN CATFISH

Prep:
20 mins
Cook:
40 mins
Total:
60 mins
Servings:
4
Yield:
4 servings

INGREDIENTS:

½ teaspoon cayenne pepper
½ teaspoon garlic powder
½ teaspoon dried dill weed
½ teaspoon dried thyme
½ teaspoon salt
½ teaspoon black pepper
4 (4 ounce) fillets catfish
¼ cup margarine, melted
1 (10 ounce) can diced tomatoes with green chile peppers, partially drained

DIRECTIONS:

1

Preheat oven to 350 degrees F (175 degrees C). Lightly grease a medium baking dish.

2

In a medium bowl, mix the cayenne pepper, garlic powder, dill weed, thyme, salt, and pepper.

3

Brush catfish fillets with the margarine, and dip into the spice mixture to coat.

4

Arrange catfish fillets in the prepared baking dish, and bake 30 minutes in the preheated oven. Top with the partially drained diced tomatoes with green chile peppers, and continue baking 10 minutes, until fish is easily flaked with a fork.

NUTRITION FACTS:

267 calories; protein 18.4g; carbohydrates 3.4g; fat 20g; cholesterol 53.4mg; sodium 763.6mg.

MEXICAN PAELLA WITH CAULIFLOWER RICE

Prep:
10 mins
Cook:
45 mins
Total:
55 mins
Servings:
8

INGREDIENTS:

1 pound chorizo sausage
1 skinless, boneless chicken breast
3 cups cauliflower rice, divided
1 medium onion, diced
1 large yellow or orange bell pepper, seeded and chopped
1 pinch salt
ground black pepper to taste
3 cloves garlic, finely minced
1 (14.5 ounce) can Hunt's® Diced Tomatoes
2 bay leaves
1 ½ teaspoons fresh thyme leaves
½ teaspoon crushed saffron threads
½ teaspoon dried basil
½ cup water
2 tablespoons tomato paste

2 cubes chicken bouillon
1 cup frozen peas
3 frozen tilapia fillets

DIRECTIONS:

1

Place paella pan or large flat-bottomed pan over medium-high heat. Cook and crumble chorizo sausage, stirring to break up chunks, until browned, about 5 minutes.
Add chicken; cook and stir with sausage
until chicken is no longer pink instead and is browned. Transfer chicken and sausage to a plate.

2

Reduce heat to medium and add 2 cups of the cauliflower rice. Cook, stirring for 5 minutes to brown the cauliflower slightly (this brings out a nutty flavor). Add the diced onion and bell pepper. Season with a pinch of salt, and pepper to taste. Add the minced garlic. Cook 2 minutes longer.

3

Pour canned tomatoes into pan. Add bay leaves, thyme leaves, saffron, and basil. Mix well. Transfer sausage and chicken mixture back to pan. Add water, tomato paste, and bouillon. Stir to combine all ingredients. Bring to a boil; reduce heat to medium-low and cover. Simmer 15 minutes.

4

Remove lid and fold in peas and remaining 1 cup of cauliflower rice. Place frozen tilapia filets on top of the paella mixture, cover and steam for another 10 minutes. Remove lid and check for doneness. Gently break apart fillets with wooden spoon, and stir to incorporate chunks of fish into paella.

5

Serve from the pot at the table!

NUTRITION FACTS:

368 calories; protein 28.6g; carbohydrates 12.2g; fat 22.7g; cholesterol 73.9mg; sodium 1244.3mg.

MEXICAN SHAKSHUKA

Prep:
10 mins
Cook:
20 mins
Total:
30 mins
Servings:
6
Yield:
6 servings

INGREDIENTS:

2 tablespoons vegetable oil
1 cup diced onion
1 tablespoon minced garlic
1 (8 ounce) jar roasted red bell peppers, drained and chopped
3 tablespoons Hunt's® Tomato Paste
1 teaspoon chili powder
1 teaspoon ground ancho chile powder
1 teaspoon ground cumin
1 teaspoon Spanish paprika
2 (14.5 ounce) cans Tomatoes, undrained
½ cup water
salt and pepper to taste
6 eggs, or more as needed

DIRECTIONS:

1

Heat oil in skillet over medium heat. Saute onions until translucent and tender, about 5 minutes.
Add chopped roasted pepper and garlic; saute until garlic releases its fragrance, 1 or 2 minutes longer. Stir in tomato paste, chili powder and ancho chili powder, cumin, and paprika. Saute for another minute or so until well combined.

2

Stir in Hunt's® Diced Tomatoes and water. Season with salt and pepper. Raise heat to medium-high and bring mixture to a boil. Immediately reduce heat to medium and cook about 5 minutes.

3

Reduce heat to medium-low. Make a well for each egg and pour 1 egg into each well. Cover; poach until whites are firm and yolks have thickened but are not hard, 2 1/2 to 5 minutes.

NUTRITION FACTS:

161 calories; protein 8g; carbohydrates 13.1g; fat 9.4g; cholesterol 163.7mg; sodium 685.3mg.

MEXICAN POTATO SAUSAGE CASSEROLE

Prep:
20 mins
Cook:
1 hr
Additional:
10 mins
Total:
1 hr 30 mins
Servings:
6
Yield:
6 servings

INGREDIENTS:

12 ounces ground chorizo or Italian sausage
½ cup chopped green bell pepper
1 (20 ounce) package Hash Browns
2 cups shredded Monterey Jack or Cheddar cheese
4 each eggs
1 cup milk
1 medium tomato, seeded, chopped

DIRECTIONS:

1

Heat oven to 350 degrees F. Spray 8 or 9-inch square baking dish with nonstick cooking spray. In 10-inch skillet cook sausage and green pepper over medium-high heat 8 to 10 minutes or until sausage is browned and cooked through; drain.

2

Place half of the Simply Potatoes in prepared baking dish. Top with half of the sausage and 3/4 cup of cheese; repeat.

3

Combine eggs and milk in medium bowl; beat well with fork. Pour egg mixture evenly over layered mixture in pan. Cover with foil; bake for 45 minutes. Uncover; add chopped tomato and remaining 1/2 cup cheese. Bake, uncovered, for an additional 10 to 15 minutes or until knife inserted in center comes out clean.

4

Let stand 10 minutes before serving.

NUTRITION FACTS:

504 calories; protein 29.5g; carbohydrates 12.9g; fat 36.9g; cholesterol 195.8mg; sodium 1155mg.

BAKED MEXICAN CHIPS ON A STICK

Prep:
15 mins
Cook:
17 mins
Total:
32 mins
Servings:
6
Yield:
6 servings

INGREDIENTS:

nonfat cooking spray
2 russet potatoes, unpeeled
2 teaspoons taco seasoning mix, or to taste
6 bamboo skewers
2 teaspoons sriracha sauce, or to taste
1 pinch sea salt to taste

DIRECTIONS:

1
Preheat oven to 425 degrees F (220 degrees C). Line a baking sheet with aluminum foil and grease with cooking spray.

2
Slice each potato into long spirals using a spiralizer fitted with the straight-flat blade. Cut each spiral into 3 shorter pieces.

3
Thread a skewer through the middle of each potato spiral. Gently push down to fan out spiral.

4
Set skewers on the prepared baking sheet; spray generously with cooking spray. Sprinkle taco seasoning on top.

5
Roast in the preheated oven until browned and crisp, 17 to 18 minutes. Season with sriracha sauce and sea salt.

NUTRITION FACTS:

59 calories; protein 1.4g; carbohydrates 13.3g; fat 0.1g; sodium 206.1mg.

ORIGINAL MEXICAN SHRIMP COCKTAIL

Prep:
30 mins
Additional:
1 hr
Total:
1 hr 30 mins
Servings:
4
Yield:
4 servings

INGREDIENTS:

4 roma (plum) tomatoes, diced
1 cup sweet onion, diced
½ cup ketchup
½ cup tomato and clam juice cocktail
½ cup prepared salsa
3 tablespoons chopped fresh cilantro
2 tablespoons prepared salsa verde
2 teaspoons lime juice
2 teaspoons hot pepper sauce
1 clove garlic, minced
1 pound frozen cooked shrimp - thawed, peeled, and deveined
2 ripe avocados - peeled, pitted, and cubed

DIRECTIONS:

1

Mix roma tomatoes, sweet onion, ketchup, tomato and clam juice cocktail, salsa, cilantro, salsa verde, lime juice, hot pepper sauce, and garlic in a glass salad bowl; cover and refrigerate until cold, about 1 hour. Cut tails from shrimp, if present, and gently fold into tomato mixture; stir avocado into shrimp cocktail.

NUTRITION FACTS:

333 calories; protein 22.8g; carbohydrates 28.7g; fat 16g; cholesterol 172.6mg; sodium 934.9mg.

MEXICAN STEAK AND VEGGIE SALAD

Prep:
25 mins
Cook:
21 mins
Additional:
2 hrs 10 mins
Total:
2 hrs 56 mins
Servings:
6

INGREDIENTS:

2 pounds flank steak
6 tablespoons extra-virgin olive oil
¼ cup lime juice
2 tablespoons Worcestershire sauce
4 cloves garlic, minced
2 teaspoons dried oregano
1 teaspoon kosher salt
¼ teaspoon ground cumin
¼ teaspoon ground black pepper
cooking spray
1 (15 ounce) can black beans, rinsed and drained
1 ½ cups cherry tomatoes
1 red onion, chopped
8 cups chopped romaine lettuce
1 cup crumbled queso fresco
¼ cup chopped fresh cilantro

DIRECTIONS:

1

Put steak in a large resealable plastic bag. Whisk olive oil, lime juice, Worcestershire sauce, garlic, oregano, salt, cumin, and black pepper in a small bowl. Reserve 1/2 cup marinade for vegetables; pour remainder over steak and turn to coat. Seal bag. Chill at least 2 hours or up to 12 hours.

2

Preheat oven to 450 degrees F (230 degrees C). Place 1 rack in center position and another 4 inches from broiler. Line a baking sheet with aluminum foil and spray with cooking spray.

3

Toss black beans, tomatoes, and onion, with reserved 1/2 cup marinade on the prepared baking sheet and spread in an even layer.

4

Roast on center rack until vegetables begin to pucker and brown, 15 to 20 minutes.

5

Remove baking sheet from oven and turn oven to broil. Push vegetables to the middle of the pan. Remove steak from marinade, allowing excess liquid to drip off, brush off garlic, and set on top of vegetables. Discard marinade.

6

Broil steak on top rack, flipping once, until it begins to char and an instant-read thermometer inserted into thickest part registers 125 degrees F (52 degrees C) for rare or 135 degrees F (57 degrees F) for medium-rare, 3 to 5 minutes per side.

7
Cover steak loosely with foil and let rest 10 minutes before slicing thinly across the grain. Serve warm steak and vegetables with pan juices over romaine; top with queso fresco and cilantro.

NUTRITION FACTS:

460 calories; protein 28.8g; carbohydrates 23g; fat 28.5g; cholesterol 60.9mg; sodium 759.4mg.

BURRITOS WITH MEXICAN CHORIZO AND POTATOES

Prep:
15 mins
Cook:
30 mins
Total:
45 mins
Servings:
8
Yield:
8 burritos

INGREDIENTS:

12 ounces Mexican chorizo, crumbled
1 medium onion, chopped
2 large potatoes, peeled and cut into small cubes
¼ cup water
1 clove garlic, crushed
8 flour tortillas, warmed

DIRECTIONS:

1

Combine chorizo and onion in a large skillet over medium heat. Cook and stir until onion is soft, about 5 minutes. Add potatoes, water, and garlic; stir well. Cover and reduce heat to medium-low. Cook, stirring every 10 minutes, until potatoes are tender, about 25 minutes. Remove from heat and spoon into warm tortillas.

NUTRITION FACTS:

354 calories; protein 12.9g; carbohydrates 45.7g; fat 13.1g; cholesterol 36.4mg; sodium 574.8mg.

CHILI-LIME SHRIMP FAJITAS

Prep:
20 mins
Cook:
16 mins
Additional:
20 mins
Total:
56 mins
Servings:
4

INGREDIENTS:

½ cup olive oil
½ cup chopped fresh cilantro, divided
3 tablespoons chili powder
4 large cloves garlic, minced
1 tablespoon lime juice
½ teaspoon salt
1 pound frozen shrimp - thawed, peeled, deveined, and cleaned
cooking spray
1 onion, sliced into rings and rings separated
1 large green bell pepper, sliced into strips
1 serrano chile pepper, sliced, or more to taste
4 (8 inch) flour tortillas
1 cup shredded Cheddar cheese, or to taste
½ cup shredded lettuce, or to taste
¼ cup sour cream, or to taste
¼ cup chopped tomatoes, or to taste

DIRECTIONS:

1

Whisk olive oil, 1/4 cup cilantro, chili powder, garlic, lime juice, and salt together in a bowl; add shrimp, toss to coat, and marinate in the refrigerator for 20 minutes.

2

Heat a large skillet over medium-high heat; spray with cooking spray. Add onion, green bell pepper, and serrano chile pepper; saute until tender, 10 to 12 minutes. Transfer vegetables to a bowl and cover with aluminum foil to keep warm.

3

Pour shrimp and marinade into the same skillet over medium-high heat; cook until shrimp are pink and opaque, about 2 minutes per side. Stir vegetables into shrimp mixture; cook and stir until heated through, 2 to 3 minutes.

4

Spoon shrimp-vegetable mixture onto tortillas and top each with Cheddar cheese, lettuce, sour cream, tomatoes, and remaining 1/4 cup cilantro.

NUTRITION FACTS:

693 calories; protein 32.6g; carbohydrates 41.5g; fat 45.1g; cholesterol 208.6mg; sodium 975.2mg.

CALABACITAS GUISADA

Prep:
10 mins
Cook:
15 mins
Additional:
5 mins
Total:
30 mins
Servings:
8
Yield:
8 servings

INGREDIENTS:

1 tablespoon vegetable oil
½ small white onion, sliced thinly
2 cloves garlic, minced
4 zucchini, sliced 1/4-inch thick
1 (14 ounce) can stewed tomatoes
salt to taste
1 cup shredded mild Cheddar cheese

DIRECTIONS:

1

Heat the vegetable oil in a saucepan over medium heat; cook the onion and garlic in the hot oil until soft, about 5 minutes.
Add the zucchini slices
and stewed tomatoes and stir gently.
Cover and cook until the zucchini is tender, 8 to 10 minutes. Remove from heat, season with salt, and add the Cheddar cheese; allow to sit until the cheese has melted.

NUTRITION FACTS:

97 calories; protein 4.8g; carbohydrates 5.8g; fat 6.6g; cholesterol 14.8mg; sodium 202.2mg

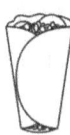

MEXICAN PORK CHILI

Prep:
30 mins
Cook:
4 hrs
Additional:
15 mins
Total:
4 hrs 45 mins
Servings:
12

INGREDIENTS:

1 ½ pounds fresh tomatillos, or more to taste, husks removed
3 serrano peppers
4 cloves garlic, peeled
1 tablespoon olive oil
3 tablespoons lard
3 pounds pork shoulder, or more to taste, trimmed and cut into 1 1/2-inch cubes
2 teaspoons garlic salt
½ teaspoon ground black pepper
1 medium yellow onion, coarsely chopped
1 green bell pepper, coarsely chopped
½ cup red wine
1 cup low-sodium chicken stock
⅓ cup chopped fresh cilantro
1 teaspoon dried oregano
1 teaspoon ground cumin

1 teaspoon kosher salt

DIRECTIONS:

1
Preheat the oven to 350 degrees F (175 degrees C).

2
Combine tomatillos, serrano peppers,
and garlic in a bowl. Drizzle with olive oil and toss to coat.
Transfer to a baking sheet.

3
Place in the preheated oven and roast until tender, about 30 minutes. Remove vegetables from oven, cool slightly, and transfer to the bowl of a food processor. Puree until smooth. Reduce oven temperature to 275 degrees F (135 degrees C).

4
While vegetables are roasting, heat lard in a Dutch oven or heavy oven-safe pot over medium-high heat. Sprinkle pork with garlic salt and pepper and add to the pot in batches. Cook each batch until browned, about 7 minutes, removing to a plate with a slotted spoon. Drain and discard all but 2 tablespoons pan drippings.

5
Add onion and bell pepper to the pot. Saute, stirring occasionally, until onion has softened and turned translucent, about 5 minutes. Pour wine into the pan and bring to a boil while scraping the browned bits of food off the bottom of the
pan with a wooden spoon. Stir in browned pork,
tomatillo puree, chicken stock, cilantro, oregano,
cumin, and salt.

6

Cover and cook in the oven until pork is tender, 3 1/2 to 4 hours. Allow to stand for 15 minutes, covered, before serving.

NUTRITION FACTS:

221 calories; protein 12.7g; carbohydrates 5.7g; fat 15.6g; cholesterol 48mg; sodium 508mg.

MEXICAN TURKEY BURGERS

Prep:
20 mins
Cook:
25 mins
Total:
45 mins
Servings:
6
Yield:
6 servings

INGREDIENTS:

1 tablespoon olive oil
1 medium onion, finely chopped
1 medium green bell pepper, finely chopped
2 cloves garlic, minced
1 cup salsa
1 (15.25 ounce) can whole kernel corn, drained
1 pound ground turkey
1 (1.25 ounce) package taco seasoning mix
⅓ cup dry bread crumbs
6 (10 inch) flour tortillas
6 tablespoons sour cream
2 cups shredded lettuce

DIRECTIONS:

tep 1
Preheat oven to 450 degrees F (230 degrees C). Coat a medium baking dish with cooking spray.

2
Heat the olive oil in a skillet over medium heat, and saute the onion, green pepper, and garlic 5 minutes. Remove from heat, and cool slightly.

3
In a small bowl, mix the salsa and 1/2 the corn. In a large bowl, mix the onion mixture with the turkey, taco seasoning, and 2 tablespoons of the salsa mixture. Divide into 6 patties, and press into the breadcrumbs to lightly coat on all sides. Arrange coated patties in the prepared baking dish.

4
Bake the patties 10 minutes in the preheated oven. Drain any liquid from the dish, turn patties, and spread with the remaining salsa mixture. Continue baking 10 minutes, to an internal temperature of 165 degrees F (75 degrees C).

5
Warm the tortillas in the microwave, about 30 seconds on High. Wrap the cooked turkey patties in the warmed tortillas with sour cream and lettuce. Sprinkle with remaining corn to serve.

NUTRITION FACTS:

509 calories; protein 25.2g; carbohydrates 64.5g; fat 17.5g; cholesterol 62.2mg; sodium 1445.2mg.

SOPA DE TORTILLA

Prep:
30 mins
Cook:
44 mins
Total:
74 mins
Servings:
4
Yield:
4 servings

INGREDIENTS:

vegetable oil, or as needed
12 (6 inch) corn tortillas, cut into strips
3 dried pasilla chile peppers, seeded
2 tomatoes, seeded and chopped
½ large onion, chopped
1 clove garlic
¼ teaspoon dried oregano
4 cups water
4 teaspoons chicken bouillon granules
1 sprig fresh parsley
1 avocado - peeled, pitted, and diced
¾ cup diced cotija cheese
2 tablespoons crema fresca (fresh cream) (Optional)

DIRECTIONS:

1
Heat oil in a large pan or wok over medium-high heat. Add tortilla strips in batches and fry until brown and crispy, 2 to 3 minutes per batch. Remove from heat and drain on paper towels.

2
Fry pasilla chiles in the same pan, being careful not to burn them, until browned, about 2 minutes. Remove from oil and drain on paper towels.

3
Combine 1 fried pasilla pepper, tomatoes, onion, garlic, and oregano in a blender; blend until smooth. Strain through a sieve into a bowl.

4
Heat 1 teaspoon oil in a saucepan over medium heat. Add tomato mixture and cook for 2 minutes. Pour in water and bring to a boil. Stir in chicken granules and parsley. Cover and simmer over low heat until flavors are well combined, about 15 minutes. Remove from heat and discard parsley.

5
Divide fried tortilla strips among 4 bowls. Pour soup on top of tortilla strips and garnish with diced avocado and cotija cheese. Cut remaining fried pasilla peppers into thin strips and sprinkle over soup. Add Mexican crema to each bowl.

NUTRITION FACTS:

606 calories; protein 13.1g; carbohydrates 49.5g; fat 42.4g;

VEGAN MEXICAN MENUDO

Prep:
10 mins
Cook:
40 mins
Additional:
5 mins
Total:
55 mins
Servings:
4
Yield:
4 cups

INGREDIENTS:

4 Roma tomatoes
2 ancho chile peppers, seeded and deveined
2 tablespoons olive oil
2 garlic cloves
1 pinch ground cumin
2 pounds shiitake mushrooms, sliced
½ cup water
salt to taste
1 quart vegetable broth

GARNISH:

¼ cup finely chopped white onion
¼ teaspoon dried oregano
1 lime, cut in wedges
1 teaspoon red pepper flakes

DIRECTIONS:

1

Place tomatoes and ancho peppers in a pot, cover with water, and bring to a boil. Cook until tender, about 5 minutes. Let soak in the hot water for 5 minutes more.

2

Transfer tomatoes, ancho peppers, and 1/2 cup water into a blender. Cover and hold lid down with a potholder; pulse a few times before leaving on to blend. Strain sauce through a sieve, discarding the solids.

3

Heat oil in a saucepan over medium heat. Crush garlic with cumin in a bowl and add to the hot pan. Cook and stir until fragrant, about 1 minute. Add mushrooms; cook and stir until soft, about 5 minutes. Pour tomato sauce over the mushrooms and season with salt. Let simmer until sauce is slightly thickened, about 5 minutes. Add vegetable broth. Bring to a boil. Reduce heat and let soup simmer until flavors meld, about 15 minutes.

4

Pour soup into individual bowls; garnish with onion and oregano. Serve with lime wedges and red pepper flakes on the side.

NUTRITION FACTS:

214 calories; protein 7.6g; carbohydrates 25.8g; fat 7.8g; sodium 559.5mg.

SEITAN FAJITAS

Prep:
15 mins
Cook:
10 mins
Total:
25 mins
Servings:
5
Yield:
5 servings

INGREDIENTS:

3 tablespoons olive oil
1 red bell pepper, cut into strips
1 green bell pepper, cut into strips
1 yellow bell pepper, cut into strips
½ red onion, chopped
1 pound seitan, cut into strips
2 tablespoons reduced-sodium soy sauce
3 cloves garlic, minced
1 teaspoon chili powder
1 teaspoon paprika
1 teaspoon ground cumin
10 whole grain tortillas

DIRECTIONS:

1
Heat oil in a large skillet over medium heat; cook and stir red bell pepper, green bell pepper, yellow bell pepper, and onion until tender, 3 to 5 minutes.
Add seitan, soy sauce, garlic, chili powder, paprika, and cumin; cook and stir until seitan is heated through, 7 to 10 minutes.

2
Spoon seitan filling onto each tortilla and fold tortilla around filling.

NUTRITION FACTS:

424 calories; protein 29.7g; carbohydrates 67.4g; fat 11.3g; sodium 924.5mg.

HOMEMADE CHICKEN FAJITAS

Prep:
25 mins
Cook:
10 mins
Additional:
5 hrs
Total:
5 hrs 35 mins
Servings:
4

INGREDIENTS:

FAJITA SEASONING:

1 tablespoon chili powder
1 teaspoon ground cumin
1 teaspoon ground paprika
1 teaspoon salt
1 teaspoon ground black pepper
¼ teaspoon cayenne pepper
¼ teaspoon garlic powder
1 ½ pounds skinless, boneless chicken breast, cut into strips
4 tablespoons olive oil, or more as needed
2 bell peppers, sliced
1 onion, thinly sliced
8 (6 inch) flour tortillas

DIRECTIONS:

1
Whisk chili powder, paprika, salt, pepper, cayenne pepper, and garlic powder for fajita seasoning together in a small bowl.

2
Trim chicken of any excess fat and place in a large, lidded bowl. Add 2 tablespoons olive oil and sprinkle with about 3/4 of the fajita seasoning. Toss, adding more oil if necessary, until coated. Poke chicken with a knife to allow penetration of seasoning and oil. Place the lid on the bowl and shake until chicken is thoroughly coated. Marinate in the refrigerator, shaking every couple of hours, for 4 to 6 hours.

3
Remove the marinating bowl from the refrigerator and let sit on the counter until chicken is room temperature, about 1 hour.

4
Preheat an outdoor grill for medium heat and lightly oil the grate. Preheat the oven to 350 degrees F (175 degrees C). Make 2 stacks of 4 tortillas, and wrap each one in aluminum foil.

5
Heat remaining 2 tablespoons olive oil in a large skillet over medium heat. Add peppers and onion. Stir in remaining fajita seasoning and cook, stirring occasionally, until vegetables are soft, 8 to 10 minutes.

6
While vegetables are cooking, place tortillas in the oven to warm. At the same time, grill chicken, turning halfway through, until no longer pink in the center and the juices run clear, 2 to 3 minutes per side.

7
To assemble fajitas, fill warmed tortillas with chicken, peppers, and onions.

NUTRITION FACTS:

560 calories; protein 42.4g; carbohydrates 43.9g; fat 23.3g; cholesterol 96.9mg; sodium 1099.1mg

RANCH-STYLE FAJITAS

Prep:
15 mins
Cook:
15 mins
Additional:
6 hrs
Total:
6 hrs 30 mins
Servings:
3
Yield:
3 servings

INGREDIENTS:

1 pound beef flank steak
¼ cup vegetable oil
3 tablespoons lime juice
1 (1 ounce) package ranch dressing mix
¼ teaspoon ground cumin
½ teaspoon ground black pepper
3 (8 inch) flour tortillas
½ onion, sliced
½ green bell pepper, sliced

DIRECTIONS:

1

Pierce the flank steak all over with a fork, and place into a large resealable plastic zipper bag. Mix the vegetable oil, lime juice, ranch dressing mix, cumin, and black pepper in a bowl, and pour over the flank steak. Force air out of the bag, seal, and refrigerate at least 6 hours.

2

Preheat an outdoor grill for medium-high heat, and lightly oil the grate.

3

Remove the flank steak from the marinade, and shake to remove excess marinade. Grill the steak until it shows good grill marks and the inside is the desired degree of doneness, about 10 minutes. Baste each side with marinade, taking care to cook the marinade onto the outside of the steak. An instant-read thermometer inserted into the middle of the steak should read 130 degrees F (54 degrees C) for medium-rare.

4

Allow the steak to rest for about 10 minutes before slicing thinly on the diagonal. While steak is resting, grill the onion and green pepper slices until they are starting to brown, about 3 minutes per side.

5

To serve, wrap sliced steak with grilled onion and green pepper in tortillas.

NUTRITION FACTS:

501 calories; protein 23.2g; carbohydrates 38g; fat 27.9g;

VEGAN FAJITAS

Prep:
20 mins
Cook:
20 mins
Additional:
30 mins
Total:
70 mins
Servings:
6
Yield:
6 servings

INGREDIENTS:

¼ cup olive oil
¼ cup red wine vinegar
1 teaspoon dried oregano
1 teaspoon chili powder
garlic salt to taste
salt and pepper to taste
1 teaspoon white sugar
2 small zucchini, julienned
2 medium small yellow squash, julienned
1 large onion, sliced
1 green bell pepper, cut into thin strips
1 red bell pepper, cut into thin strips
2 tablespoons olive oil
1 (8.75 ounce) can whole kernel corn, drained
1 (15 ounce) can black beans, drained

DIRECTIONS:

1

In a large bowl combine olive oil, vinegar, oregano, chili powder, garlic salt, salt, pepper and sugar. To the marinade add the zucchini, yellow squash, onion, green pepper and red pepper. Marinate vegetables in the refrigerator for at least 30 minutes, but not more than 24 hours.

2

Heat oil in a large skillet over medium-high heat. Drain the vegetables and saute until tender, about 10 to 15 minutes. Stir in the corn and beans; increase the heat to high for 5 minutes, to brown vegetables.

NUTRITION FACTS:

198 calories; protein 3g; carbohydrates 17.9g; fat 14.4g; sodium 130.2mg

SHRIMP QUESADILLAS

Prep:
15 mins
Cook:
1 hr
Total:
1 hr 15 mins
Servings:
6
Yield:
6 quesadillas

INGREDIENTS:

2 tablespoons vegetable oil
1 onion, sliced
1 red bell pepper, sliced
1 green bell pepper, sliced
1 teaspoon salt
1 teaspoon ground cumin
1 teaspoon chili powder
1 pound uncooked medium shrimp, peeled and deveined
1 jalapeno pepper, seeded and minced
1 lime, juiced
1 teaspoon vegetable oil, or as needed
6 large flour tortillas
3 cups shredded Mexican cheese blend, divided

DIRECTIONS:

1
Heat 2 tablespoons vegetable oil in a large skillet over medium-high heat. Cook and stir onion, red bell pepper, and green bell pepper in the hot oil, stirring frequently, until onion is translucent and peppers are soft, 6 to 8 minutes.

2
Stir salt, cumin, and chili powder into onion and bell peppers.

3
Stir shrimp into onion and bell peppers and cook until shrimp are opaque and no longer pink in the center, 3 to 5 minutes.

4
Remove skillet from heat; stir jalapeno pepper and lime juice into shrimp mixture.

5
Heat a skillet over medium heat and brush with about 1 teaspoon vegetable oil.

6
Place a tortilla in the hot oil. Spoon about 1/6 shrimp filling and 1/2 cup Mexican cheese blend on one side of tortilla. Fold tortilla in half.

7
Cook until bottom of tortilla is lightly browned, about 5 minutes; flip and cook other side until lightly browned, 3 to 5 minutes. Repeat with remaining tortillas and filling.

NUTRITION FACTS:

753 calories; protein 37.9g; carbohydrates 67.8g; fat 36.9g; cholesterol 179.7mg; sodium 1788.4mg.

THANKSGIVING QUESADILLA

Prep:
10 mins
Cook:
5 mins
Total:
15 mins
Servings:
6
Yield:
6 Slices

INGREDIENTS:

2 flour tortillas
½ cup shredded Cheddar cheese
¼ pound shredded cooked turkey meat
2 tablespoons cranberry sauce
½ jalapeno pepper, seeded and minced
1 green onion, sliced
2 tablespoons chopped fresh cilantro, or to taste

DIRECTIONS:

1

Heat a skillet over medium heat. Place 1 tortilla in the skillet and top with 1/2 of the Cheddar cheese, turkey, cranberry sauce, jalapeno pepper, green onion, and remaining Cheddar cheese, respectively.
Place remaining tortilla over the top.

2

Cook until tortilla is golden brown and cheese is melted, 2 to 4 minutes per side.

NUTRITION FACTS:

141 calories; protein 9.9g; carbohydrates 11.6g; fat 5.9g; cholesterol 26.4mg;

CREAMY JALAPENO AND PULLED PORK QUESADILLA

Prep:
10 mins
Additional:
15 mins
Total:
25 mins
Servings:
8
Yield:
8 servings

INGREDIENTS:

4 (8 inch) flour tortillas
½ cup PHILADELPHIA Spicy Jalapeno Cream Cheese Spread
1 (11.5 ounce) package OSCAR MAYER CARVING BOARD Sweet & Spicy Pulled Pork
½ cup frozen corn, thawed
½ cup chopped red pepper
½ cup tomatillo salsa

DIRECTIONS:

1

Spread tortillas evenly with cream cheese; top half of each of tortilla with remaining ingredients. Fold tortillas in half.

2

Heat large skillet sprayed with cooking spray on medium heat. Add 1 quesadilla; cook 4 to 5 min. or until golden brown on both sides, turning after 2 to 3 min. Repeat with remaining quesadilla. Cut into wedges. Serve with salsa

HAM, EGG, AND CHEESE QUESADILLAS

Prep:
10 mins
Cook:
30 mins
Total:
40 mins
Servings:
6
Yield:
6 quesadillas

INGREDIENTS:

8 eggs
1 tablespoon water
½ teaspoon salt
½ teaspoon pepper
2 tablespoons butter, softened, divided
6 (8 inch) whole wheat tortillas
2 cups shredded Cheddar cheese
1 (8 ounce) package Cubed Ham

DIRECTIONS:

1

Scramble eggs with water, salt, and pepper in a medium bowl until well blended. Heat 1 tablespoon butter in a medium nonstick skillet over medium heat.
Cook eggs, stirring frequently,
until scrambled to desired consistency.

2

Spread 1 teaspoon of butter over 1 tortilla and place butter-side down in a medium nonstick skillet over medium heat. Sprinkle 1/3 cup cheese over entire tortilla. Add 1/2 cup scrambled egg and 1/3 cup Smithfield® cubed ham to one side. Cook 3 minutes or until the cheese is melted. Fold the plain cheese side over the filled side and flip the quesadilla. Cook an additional 2 minutes or until golden and toasted. Cut into 2 or 3 pieces.

3

Repeat with remaining ingredients to make 5 more quesadillas.

NUTRITION FACTS:

418 calories; protein 27.7g; carbohydrates 28.7g; fat 24.6g; cholesterol 317.7mg; sodium 1213.8mg.

CHICKEN QUESADILLAS

Prep:
30 mins
Cook:
25 mins
Total:
55 mins
Servings:
20
Yield:
20 servings

INGREDIENTS:

1 pound skinless, boneless chicken breast, diced
1 (1.27 ounce) packet fajita seasoning
1 tablespoon vegetable oil
2 green bell peppers, chopped
2 red bell peppers, chopped
1 onion, chopped
10 (10 inch) flour tortillas
1 (8 ounce) package shredded Cheddar cheese
1 tablespoon bacon bits
1 (8 ounce) package shredded Monterey Jack cheese

DIRECTIONS:

1
Preheat the broiler. Grease a baking sheet.

2
Toss the chicken with the fajita seasoning, then spread onto the baking sheet. Place under the broiler and cook until the chicken pieces are no longer pink in the center, about 5 minutes.

3
Preheat oven to 350 degrees F (175 degrees C).

4
Heat the oil in a large saucepan over medium heat. Stir in the green bell peppers, red bell peppers, onion, and chicken. Cook and stir until the vegetables have softened, about 10 minutes.

5
Layer half of each tortilla with the chicken and vegetable mixture, then sprinkle with the Cheddar cheese, bacon bits, and Monterey Jack. Fold the tortillas in half and Place onto a baking sheet.

6
Bake quesadillas in the preheated oven until the cheeses have melted, about 10 minutes.

NUTRITION FACTS:

244 calories; protein 13.7g; carbohydrates 21.8g; fat 11.3g; cholesterol 34.9mg; sodium 504.3mg

VEGAN BLACK BEAN QUESADILLAS

Prep:
10 mins
Cook:
45 mins
Total:
55 mins
Servings:
4
Yield:
4 servings

INGREDIENTS:

1 (15 ounce) can great Northern beans, drained and rinsed
¾ cup diced tomatoes
1 clove garlic
⅓ cup nutritional yeast
1 teaspoon ground cumin
¼ teaspoon chili powder
salt to taste
1 pinch cayenne pepper, or to taste
½ cup black beans, drained and rinsed
¼ cup diced tomatoes
1 tablespoon olive oil, or as needed
8 whole grain tortillas
cooking spray

DIRECTIONS:

1

Blend great Northern beans, 3/4 cup tomatoes, and garlic in a food processor until smooth; add nutritional yeast, cumin, chili powder, salt, and red pepper flakes and blend again.

2

Transfer bean mixture to a bowl. Stir black beans and 1/4 cup tomatoes into bean mixture.

3

Heat olive oil in a skillet over medium-high heat.

4

Place a tortilla in the hot oil. Spread about 1/4 cup filling onto the tortilla.

5

Place another tortilla on top of filling; cook until filling is warmed, about 10 minutes.

6

Spray the top tortilla with cooking spray and flip quesadilla to cook the second side until lightly browned, 3 to 5 minutes. Repeat with remaining tortillas and filling.

NUTRITION FACTS:

416 calories; protein 23.2g; carbohydrates 85.6g; fat 5.8g; sodium 616.4mg.

JALAPENO AND CANADIAN BACON BREAKFAST QUESADILLAS

Prep:
15 mins
Cook:
10 mins
Additional:
5 mins
Total:
30 mins

INGREDIENTS:

3 tablespoons unsalted butter, divided
2 jalapeno peppers, seeded and chopped
3 slices Jones Dairy Farm Canadian Bacon, chopped
4 large eggs
2 tablespoons whole milk
1 teaspoon extra virgin olive oil
1 pinch sea salt
1 cup shredded Mexican blend cheese, divided
2 ounces cream cheese, softened
2 flour tortillas
2 green onions, sliced
1 tablespoon Sour cream
¼ teaspoon Salsa

DIRECTIONS:

1
In non-stick omelet pan, melt 1 tablespoon butter over medium heat.

2
Add peppers and cook for 2-3 minutes, tossing frequently. Add Canadian Bacon and cook for another 1-2 minutes, tossing frequently. Remove to paper-towel lined plate.

3
In medium mixing bowl, whisk together eggs and milk, beating until frothy.

4
Wipe out omelet pan, add 1 tablespoon butter and extra virgin olive oil to pan and heat over medium low heat.

5
Once butter is melted, pour in eggs. Sprinkle sea salt over eggs and let sit for about 3 minutes, adjusting temperature as necessary to ensure a low, slow cook without burning the bottom. Once sides are set but middle is still wet, sprinkle 1/3 cup cheese, peppers and Canadian Bacon over eggs. Cook for 1 minute, then loosen edges with silicone spatula and flip eggs. Aim for mostly one large piece of egg, any cracks will slightly repair when other side cooks. Cook until bottom is set, 2-3 minutes, then slide onto plate and set aside.

6
Spread cream cheese over tortillas.

7
Place cast iron skillet over medium heat and add 1/2 tablespoon butter. Once melted, place prepared tortilla in pan, cream cheese side up. Sprinkle 1/3 cup cheese over entire surface and place half of the eggs over one half of tortilla. Sprinkle half of green onions over eggs.
Cook over medium to medium-low heat until cheese is melted, then fold in half.

8
Remove to cutting board and let sit for 1-2 minutes before slicing. Repeat with other tortilla and remaining eggs. Serve with sour cream and salsa.

NUTRITION FACTS:

839 calories; protein 37.6g; carbohydrates 34g; fat 62g; cholesterol 517.1mg; sodium 1310.1mg.

APPLE-CINNAMON BURRITO

Prep:
5 mins
Cook:
5 mins
Additional:
15 mins
Total:
25 mins
Servings:
1
Yield:
1 burrito

INGREDIENTS:

1 medium apple - peeled, cored, and sliced
2 teaspoons water
½ tablespoon unsalted butter
2 teaspoons brown sugar
½ teaspoon ground cinnamon
1 (8 inch) flour tortilla
2 scoops vanilla ice cream

DIRECTIONS:

1

Place apple slices and water in a microwave-safe bowl and cover tightly with plastic wrap. Microwave on high power until apple slices are soft, about 3 minutes.

2

Mix butter, brown sugar, and cinnamon in another microwave-safe bowl. Microwave in 30-second intervals, stirring after each interval, until melted and the consistency is of a thick liquid. Spread on tortilla and lay apple down the middle. Place in the refrigerator until cool, about 15 minutes.

3

Remove from the refrigerator and place ice cream on top of apples. Wrap tortilla as you would wrap a burrito.

NUTRTION FACTS:

404 calories; protein 6.2g; carbohydrates 66.2g; fat 14.1g; cholesterol 33.7mg; sodium 273mg.

GARBANZO BEAN AND VEGGIE BURRITOS

Prep:
10 mins
Cook:
25 mins

INGREDIENTS:

1 ½ tablespoons olive oil
½ large onion, diced
3 cloves garlic, minced, or more to taste
2 tomatoes, divided
2 (15 ounce) cans garbanzo beans, drained
2 tablespoons lemon juice, divided
2 teaspoons olive oil, divided
1 ½ teaspoons butter
2 zucchini, chopped
1 yellow squash, chopped
1 green bell pepper, diced
salt and ground black pepper to taste
1 ½ teaspoons ground cumin
1 teaspoon chili powder
1 teaspoon paprika
6 (10 inch) flour tortillas
½ cup shredded Cheddar cheese (Optional)
1 dash hot sauce, or to taste (Optional)

DIRECTIONS:

1

Heat 1 1/2 tablespoons olive oil in a skillet over medium heat; cook and stir onion and garlic until onion is translucent, 5 to 10 minutes. Add 1/2 of the chopped tomatoes; cook and stir for 1 minute. Add garbanzo beans, 1 tablespoon lemon juice, and 1 teaspoon olive oil; cover skillet and cook, stirring occasionally, until heated through, about 10 minutes.

2

Heat butter and remaining 1 teaspoon olive oil in a separate skillet over medium heat; cook and stir zucchini, yellow squash, and green bell pepper until tender, about 5 minutes. Season with salt and black pepper.

3

Mix remaining 1 tablespoon lemon juice into garbanzo bean mixture; cover and cook for 5 minutes more. Mash garbanzo beans with a potato masher while skillet is still over heat until desired consistency is reach. Mix cumin, chili powder, and paprika into garbanzo beans; stir to coat.

4

Layer garbanzo bean mixture, vegetable mixture, and remaining tomatoes onto each tortilla; top with Cheddar cheese and hot sauce. Fold opposing edges of the tortilla to overlap the filling.
Roll 1 of the opposing edges around the filling into a burrito.

NUTRITION FACTS:

457 calories; protein 14.5g; carbohydrates 65.1g; fat 16.1g; cholesterol 12.6mg; sodium 833.8mg

www.ingramcontent.com/pod-product-compliance
Lightning Source LLC
Chambersburg PA
CBHW070930080526
44589CB00013B/1464